SILENT AS A STONE

Mother Maria of Paris and the Trash Can Rescue

JIM FOREST

illustrated by Dasha Pancheshnaya

ST VLADIMIR'S SEMINARY PRESS • CRESTWOOD • NEW YORK • 2007

In the chapel of a house on Rue de Lourmel, a nun stood in front of a candlelit icon. "Dear Lord," she prayed, "give me strength. Paris has become a prison."

Tears shone on her round face and fell onto her tattered robe. Mother Maria turned to the flame that danced beneath an image of the Christ child in his mother's protective arms. Again, she begged, "Mother of God and Lord Jesus, they are arresting your people and sending them away. We don't know where. Help us to help them!"

It was a prayer Mother Maria had said countless times since that black day two years before when Paris had surrendered to the German army. War had turned her beautiful city into a place of danger, particularly for the Jewish people. German soldiers now patrolled the streets outside her doorstep.

There was a quiet knocking on the chapel door—a signal from her friend, Father Dimitri, when he needed to interrupt her prayers.

"Mother Maria," said the young priest, "I'm sorry, but please come."

Crossing the courtyard silently, Mother Maria dried her face.

Jérémy, one of the neighborhood children, stood just inside the kitchen door, eyes wide. "Mother Maria, they took Papa and Mama and Esther! Papa got me out by the window just before they broke down the door. I hid in the alley."

As Jérémy sobbed, Mother Maria reached out and cradled his thin body that seemed too small for such grief. She remembered holding her own little boy, Yuri, so many years before. Now Yuri was grown, and she had left married life behind to be a nun. Together they served the homeless and penniless of Paris—and, now, the Jews.

She reassured Jérémy, "We will find your family. Somehow we will find them. I promise."

Jérémy's eyes closed in exhaustion. Father Dimitri carried him to a bed upstairs.

A knock came at the kitchen door... then another. Neighbors filled the kitchen. All had similar news—arrests in the night, arrests still going on, Jews being taken away, thousands of Jews. But where?

Mother Maria's son, Yuri, pushed into the crowded room. He was breathless from running.

"Mother," cried Yuri, "they are filling the Vél d'Hiv with thousands of Jews! More and more buses full of Jews keep arriving at the stadium. Police and soldiers are everywhere."

Mother Maria took Yuri's arm and together they walked briskly through the busy city streets to the stadium entrance.

Two French policemen blocked their way. "No one is allowed to enter," one explained.

"Shame on you for being part of all this!" scolded Mother Maria. "What harm have these people done? But surely you won't deprive them of spiritual comfort! Let me in so I can at least give them a kind word."

The policemen exchanged embarrassed glances, then stood aside. "All right, but only you, not the boy," said the taller of the men. "And take care you do nothing to irritate the Germans. They're the ones running the show."

The locked gate was opened. "Wait for me," Mother Maria said to Yuri. "Let me see what can be done."

Mother Maria blinked back astonished tears. The Vél d'Hiv, ordinarily a stadium for bicycle races, had become a concentration camp. She spotted Jérémy's family not far from the entrance. Little Esther ran to her and asked, "Mother Maria, why are they doing this? What did we do wrong? When can we go home?"

"I don't know, my dear. It's unfair. But I will do my best to help you."

Sitting down between Esther's parents, Mother Maria looked with dismay at the growing throng. Many children were crying. Esther's mother cautiously whispered, "Have you seen Jérémy?"

"Yes, he made his way to us. He's now asleep in Father Dimitri's apartment," Mother Maria answered softly. "We will take care of him. But how can I help you?"

"We fear that for us it's hopeless," said Esther's father. "But…but our dear Esther? Is there some way you could help her to safety?"

Mother Maria was silent for a moment, but then replied, "I will try to find a way. God help us!"

For hours Mother Maria made her way among the captives in the stadium, consoling them and sharing bits of bread from her pockets. Again and again, parents begged her to save their children. Again and again, Mother Maria prayed to find a way.

In amongst the prisoners Mother Maria noticed trash collectors busy at work, filling their trash cans with garbage and hauling them away. Among them she recognized her old friend, Pierre, who collected the garbage at Rue de Lourmel.

Suddenly Mother Maria had an idea. She hurried over to Pierre.

"Mother Maria!" Pierre greeted her with a smile, but it soon faded to a pained look. "They do this dirty work, Mother Maria," said Pierre, frowning, "but they want us to keep it tidy!"

"There is something you can do to help!" Mother Maria whispered earnestly. "Every time you fill your trash can, put a child inside! Then bring the children to our house. The guards have too much to do—they'll pay no attention to the garbage."

"A dangerous plan," Pierre murmured, but at a nod of his head some of the other trash collectors gathered around. They talked quietly. Then, hitting the ground with his broom, Pierre declared, "Let's try! I'll be the first. If I manage to come back, then you try too. Let's see how many we can save."

of children by enlisting the aid of trash collectors who smuggled the children out in trash cans—until the Nazis barred her from the stadium.

Early in 1943, the long-expected event happened: Mother Maria, Yuri, and Father Dimitri were arrested and soon after were sent to the first of several concentration camps.

The final destination for Yuri and Father Dimitri was a camp named Dora. Both died there in the early months of 1944. A final letter from Yuri was discovered in a suitcase of his possessions returned to Rue de Lourmel:

"I am absolutely calm, even somewhat proud to share Mama's fate. I promise you I will bear everything with dignity. Whatever happens, sooner or later we shall all be together. I can say in all honesty that I am not afraid of anything any longer.... I ask anyone whom I have hurt in any way to forgive me. Christ be with you!"

Mother Maria was sent in a sealed cattle truck to the Ravensbrück camp in Germany, where she endured for two years. Here she managed to help those around her and even made an embroidered icon of the Mother of God holding a cross that supported her crucified Son.

One fellow prisoner recalled that Mother Maria "was never downcast, never. She was full of good cheer, really good cheer. She was on good terms with everyone. She was the kind of person who made no distinction between people no matter what their political views might be or their religious beliefs."

By March 1945, Mother Maria's condition was critical. She had to lie down between roll calls and hardly spoke. Her face, a friend recalled, "revealed intense inner suffering. Already it bore the marks of death. Nevertheless Mother Maria made no complaint. She kept her eyes closed and seemed to be in a state of continual prayer."

The last day of her life was the day before Easter. The shellfire of the approaching Russian army could be heard in the distance.

Accounts vary as to what happened during the last hours of her life. According to one account, she was simply one of those selected to die that day. According to another, she took the place of a fellow prisoner, a Jewish woman.

Although perishing in the gas chamber, Mother Maria did not perish in the Church's memory. Soon after the end of World War II, essays and books about her began appearing in French and Russian. Two biographies were published in English, and little by little her essays were made available in several languages, most recently English.

On May 1 and 2, 2004, at Saint Alexander Nevsky Cathedral in Paris, Mother Maria, her son Yuri, Father Dimitri Klépinin, and their friend and co-worker Ilya Fondaminsky were officially recognized as saints. The Holy Synod of the Patriarchate of Constantinople established the 20th of July each year as the day of their remembrance.

IMAGES

Images in the Historical Note are taken from incommunion.org, the web site of the Orthodox Peace Fellowship:

- Mother Maria in her monastic habit
- Icon of St Maria Skobtsova and fellow martyrs, by Olga Poloukhine
- The house at 77 Rue de Lourmel, Paris

FURTHER READING

Pearl of Great Price: The Life of Mother Maria Skobtsova 1891–1945, Sergei Hackel (St Vladimir's Seminary Press, 1981).

The Rebel Nun, T. Stratton Smith (Templegate, 1965).

Mother Maria Skobtsova: Essential Writings, edited by Hélène Klépinin-Arjakovsky (Orbis, 2003).

*To all our grandchildren
so far, Zachary, Kara,
Noah and Joshua.*
—J. F.

*In loving memory
of my grandfather
Gleb Ivanovich Platt.*
—D. P.

LIBRARY OF CONGRESS CATALOGING-IN-PUBLICATION DATA

Forest, James H.
  Silent as a stone : Mother Maria of Paris and the trash can rescue / Jim Forest ; illustrated by Dasha Pancheshnaya.
    p. cm.
  ISBN-13: 978-0-88141-314-4
  ISBN-10: 0-88141-314-3
1. Mariia, mat', 1891-1945—Juvenile literature. 2. Jewish children in the Holocaust—France—Paris—Juvenile literature.
3. Jews—Persecutions—France—Paris—Juvenile literature.
4. Holocaust, Jewish (1939-1945)—France—Paris—Juvenile literature. I. Pancheshnaya, Dasha. II. Title.

BX597.M3F67 2007
940.53'1835092—dc22
[B] 2007005192

ST VLADIMIR'S SEMINARY PRESS
575 Scarsdale Road, Crestwood, New York 10707
1-800-204-2665
www.svspress.com

text copyright © 2007 Jim Forest • illustrations copyright © 2007 Dasha Pancheshnaya

All rights reserved
ISBN 978-0-88141-314-4

book & cover design: Amber Schley • typeset in Hoefler Text

PRINTED IN CHINA